ROXIE MUNRO

Slithery Snakes

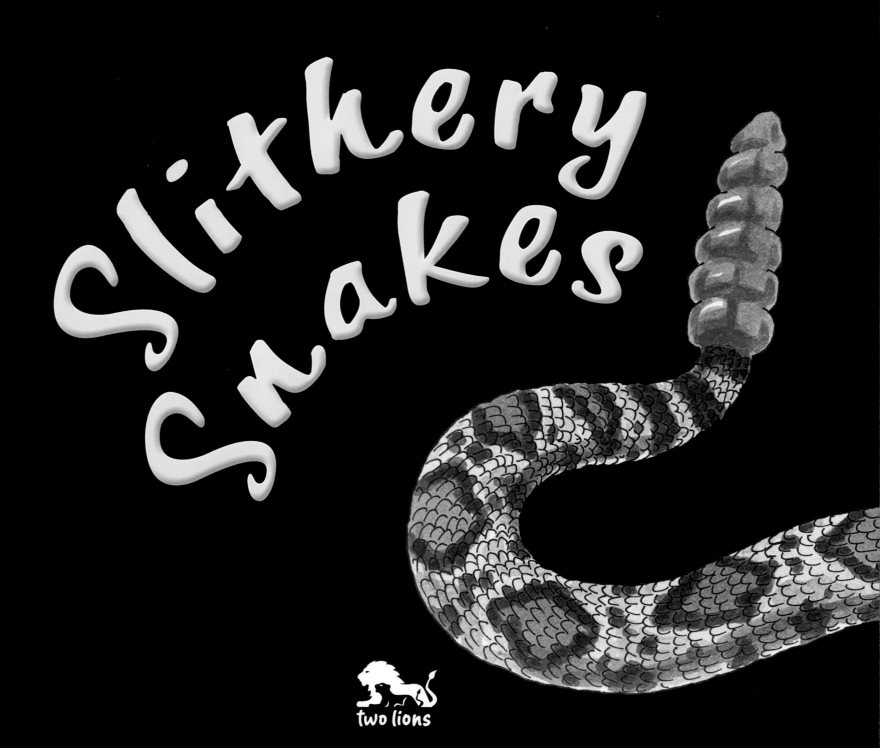

two lions

To my artist sister, Ann Munro Wood, who loves patterns and color as much as I do

Many thanks to Christopher J. Raxworthy, Associate Curator of Herpetology
at the American Museum of Natural History, for his expert review of this manuscript.

Fun Snake Facts

- The fastest snake is the African black mamba, clocked at 7 miles per hour (11 km/h). That's about as fast as you can run.
- Snake jaws are not fused (hooked) together in the back of their mouths like humans', so they can open their mouths extra wide to eat very big creatures.
- The thread snake is one of the smallest snakes at only 5 inches (13 cm) long. An anaconda is one of the largest—36 feet (11 m) long.
- Snakes swallow prey like mice headfirst so the legs won't get stuck in their throats and the claws won't scratch their throats and esophagi.
- The world's deadliest land snake is the Inland Taipan from Australia, but the beaked sea snake has the most powerful venom in the world.
- Some snakes, including sand snakes in Africa and the Middle East, perform scale polishing: they move their heads in zigzag motions down their bodies up to 100 times a day, polishing scales with a secretion from their nostrils.
- Flying snakes live in Southeastern Asian rainforests. These snakes straighten from an S-position and launch themselves off tall branches, spreading their ribs so they parachute to the ground.
- Snakes don't have external ear openings; they "hear" by feeling vibrations.
- There are no snakes in New Zealand or Ireland and few in Hawaii.
- Snakes do not have eyelids. Their eyes are covered with a clear scale called a spectacle. They have bad eyesight. But they can smell with their tongues!

two lions

Text and illustrations copyright © 2013 by Roxie Munro
Amazon Publishing
Attn: Amazon Children's Publishing
P.O. Box 400818, Las Vegas, NV 89140
www.amazon.com/amazonchildrenspublishing
Library of Congress Cataloging-in-Publication Data available upon request.
ISBN-13: 9781477816585 (hardcover), ISBN-10: 1477816585 (hardcover)
ISBN-13: 9781477866580 (eBook), ISBN-10: 1477866582 (eBook)

The illustrations are rendered in India ink and colored ink.
Book design by Anahid Hamparian. Editor: Marilyn Brigham

Printed in China (R)
First edition
10 9 8 7 6 5 4 3 2

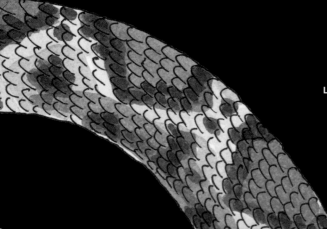

Humans have been captivated and frightened by snakes for thousands of years. In the Bible, the serpent tempts Eve with an apple. In ancient Egypt, snakes were a symbol of the sea. From Greek mythology comes the Gorgon with snakes instead of hair. Many Chinese, Indian, Hebrew, and Nordic myths involve snakes, and there are Aesop's fables about them. In North America, Hopi Indians performed a snake dance.

Snakes are cold-blooded and have evolved from lizards. They belong to the animal group Reptiles and live almost anywhere—forests, deserts, lakes, the ocean—except in very cold polar areas. There are at least 2,700 species of snakes worldwide, and about 400 are venomous. Snakes are carnivores. Venomous snakes (cobras, vipers, rattlesnakes) paralyze or maim their prey; constrictors (pythons, boas) squeeze their dinner to death. Snakes have predators, too: large birds, lizards, mammals, even other snakes. They protect themselves by using camouflage, burrowing into the earth, huffing or hissing, rattling their tails, imitating the colors of more dangerous snakes, and playing dead.

Snakes have no arms or legs, but they have strong muscles and flexible spines. They travel by sidewinding, creeping, and crawling. Their internal organs are similar to ours—but really long and skinny! Snakes have a heart, an elongated throat and esophagus, and a stretched-out tummy, liver, gall bladder, and kidneys. They breathe air into one long lung (big boas and pythons have two). Some snakes give birth to live young while others lay eggs.

Snakes may be sneaky, slithery, and scary, but they are also among nature's most intriguing, even beautiful, creatures.

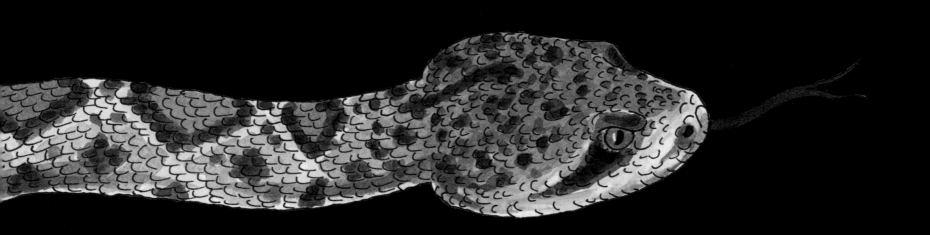

Can you guess what kind of snake this is?

Because of its stripes, this snake is named after an article of clothing men once wore to hold up their socks. Its species is spread throughout North America, and it is the only type of snake found in Alaska.

The **COAST GARTER SNAKE** *(Thamnophis elegans terrestris)* is diurnal (active during the day) and carnivorous. It eats worms, lizards, fish, snails, frogs, rodents, birds, and sometimes eggs, and lives in all sorts of habitats (woodlands, grass, dunes), usually near water. Garter snakes in the north brumate (which is like hibernating, but is not as long or deep a sleep) in large numbers in dens. They sometimes travel up to 20 miles (32 km) to reach their winter dens. After the snakes wake up and mate, they migrate—often hundreds at a time, crossing roads and highways. In the northeastern United States and Canada, humans have built "snake tunnels" under highways to protect garter snakes on their journeys.

Also in this woodlands habitat: frog, mouse, mallard duck, gray squirrel

Can you guess what kind of snake this is?

The newborn baby snake is orange or red but turns bright green after about a year. It can grow up to 9 feet (2.8 m) long and lives its whole life in trees, coming to the ground once in a while to move to another tree.

The **EMERALD TREE BOA** *(Corallus caninus)* lives in South America, mainly in the Amazon rainforest. It stays coiled or looped over a branch all day, sleeping. At night the snake extends its head downward, waiting. This boa has vertical pupils, which help it sense movement at night, and deep pits around its mouth for detecting heat from its prey. It will grab a bird or a rodent or even a monkey with its long front teeth, and because it is a constrictor, will squeeze it until it dies. Meals may be weeks apart. The moms give birth to live young, who, once they are born, are on their own.

Also in this rainforest habitat: monkey, toucan, jaguar, dragonfly

Can you guess what kind of snake this is?

This snake, a relative of the Indian cobra, has venom twice as lethal as a rattlesnake's. Different species of harmless snakes mimic the body patterns of this snake for protection from it.

Also in this desert habitat: monarch butterfly, horned lizard, turkey vulture, red-tailed hawk

To distinguish the dangerous **WESTERN CORAL SNAKE** (*Micruroideseuryxanthus*) from a harmless copycat king snake or milk snake, remember this phrase: "Red touch yellow, kill a fellow." (The deadly snakes have a yellow ring next to each red one; the copycats have black rings in between the red and yellow.) Coral snakes are in the same family as highly venomous cobras, kraits, mambas, and sea snakes. They live in the rocky deserts, woodlands, and grasslands of the southwestern United States. These snakes are small—usually less than 2 feet (60 cm) long—and are about as thick as a pencil. They hunt at night, devouring lizards and small snakes, and can be cannibals—and eat another coral snake for dinner.

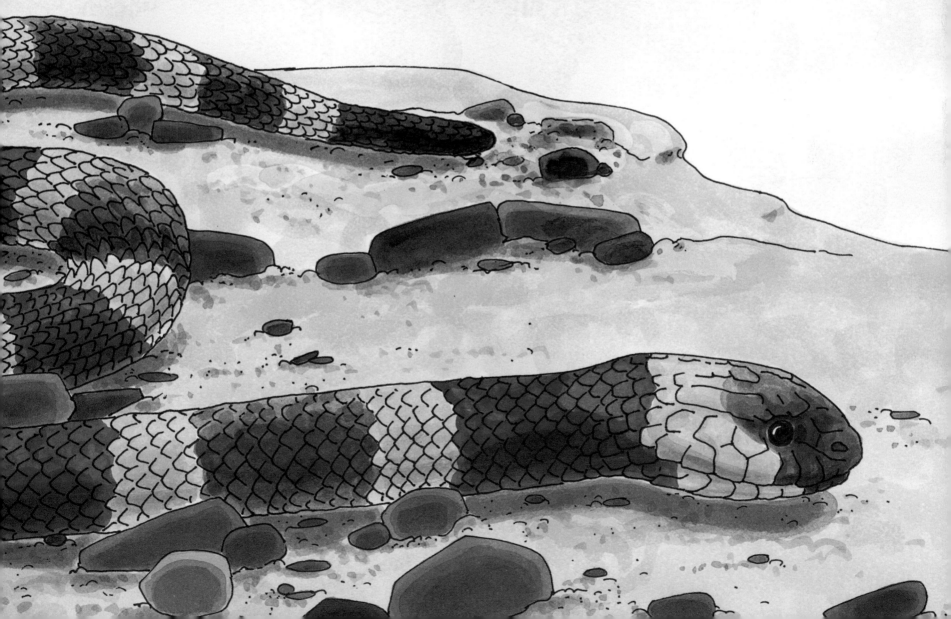

Can you guess what kind of snake this is?

This snake has elongated scales, which are brightly colored and look spiny or bristly. Its big eyes and short snout make it look almost like a cartoon.

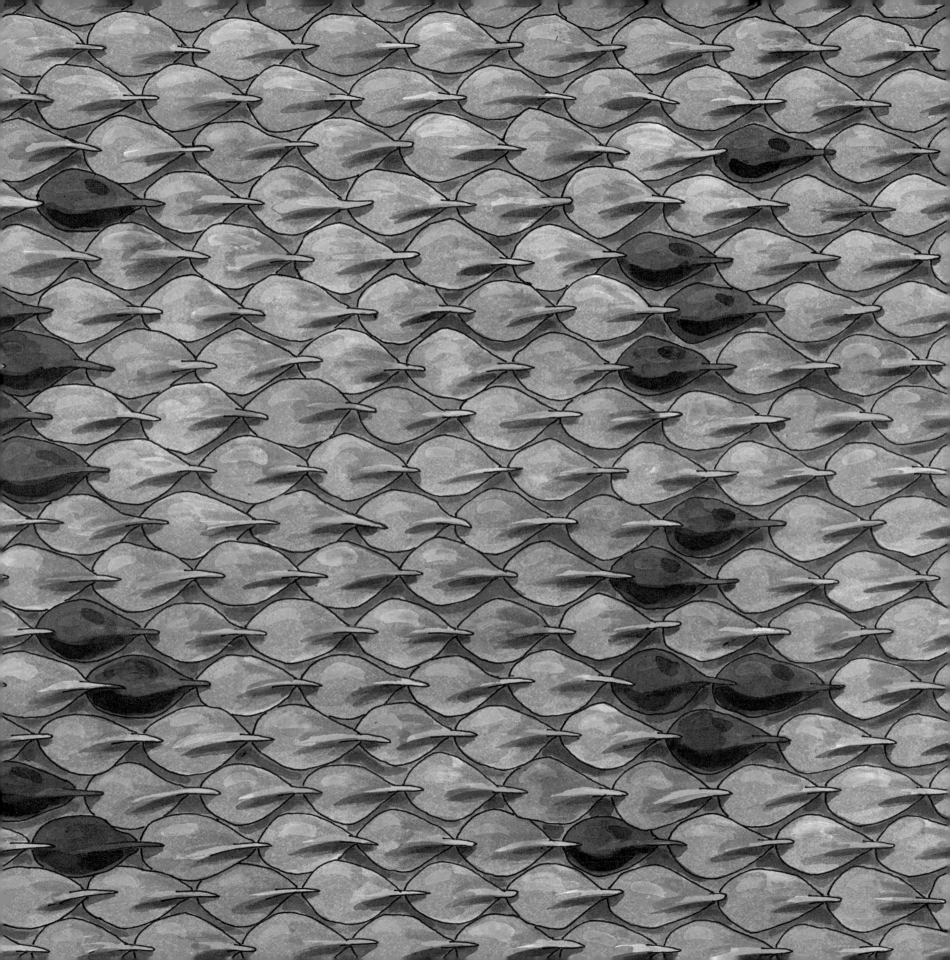

Also in this tropical forest habitat: leopard, crocodile, elephant, Cape buffalo

The **SPINY BUSH VIPER** (*Atheris hispida*) lives in central Africa. Because of its unusual scales, it is also called a hairy or rough-scaled bush viper or a feathered tree viper. A viper has 2 large, retractable, venomous fangs in the front of its upper jaw. It is mainly nocturnal, hunting at night for small mammals, frogs, lizards, and sometimes birds. The spiny bush viper is arboreal: it likes to climb bushes and reeds. Males grow to more than 2 feet (60 cm); females are smaller. Females give live birth to up to a dozen babies, which are about 10 inches (25 cm) long when they're born.

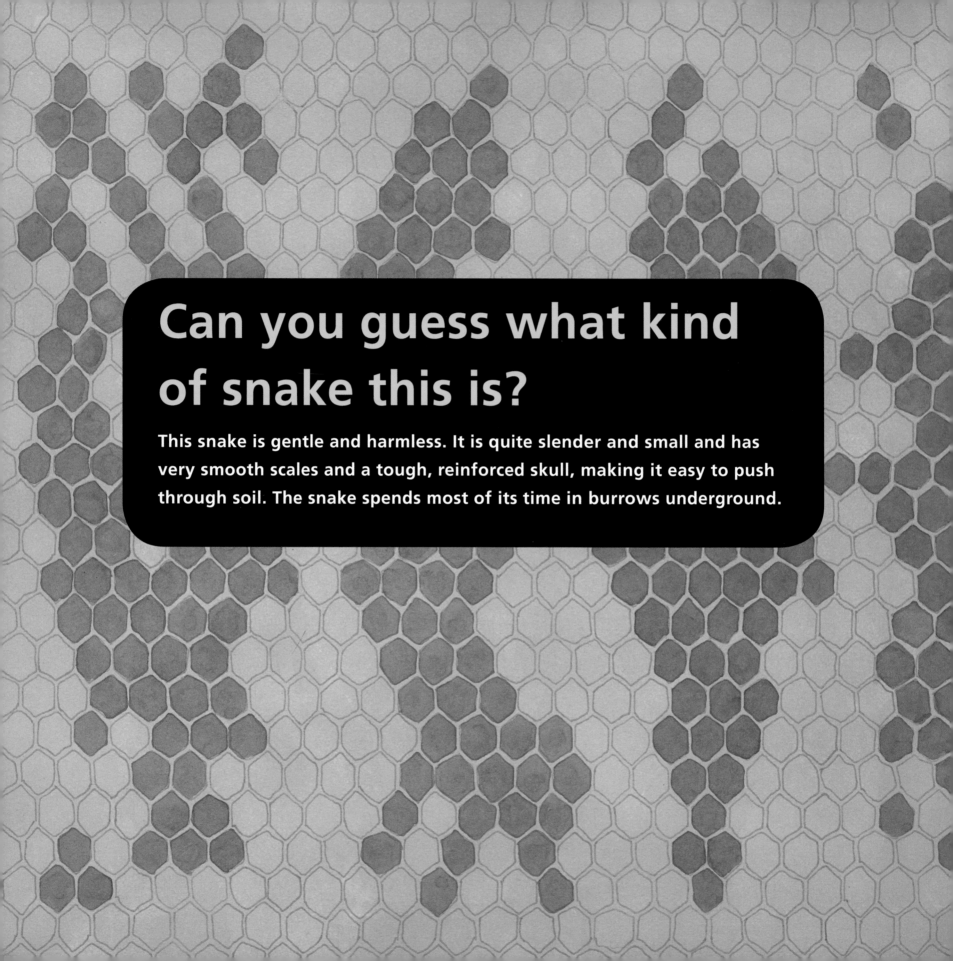

Can you guess what kind of snake this is?

This snake is gentle and harmless. It is quite slender and small and has very smooth scales and a tough, reinforced skull, making it easy to push through soil. The snake spends most of its time in burrows underground.

SCHINZ'S BEAKED BLIND SNAKE (*Rhinotyphlops schinzi*) lives in the semidesert and arid savannas of southern Africa. It has a blunt head and does have eyes—they're hidden under scales. Unlike the eyes of other snakes, the eyes of this snake are not transparent, so it can barely see. Blind snakes rely on other senses, such as touch and smell. The Schinz's beaked snake dines on termites and ants (and their larvae and pupae) and eats frequently, unlike larger snakes. It is only about 8–11 inches (20–28 cm) long. This blind snake is preyed upon by other snakes. It can't bite; but to defend itself it will release a nasty smell, wiggle wildly, and even poke the predator with its tail.

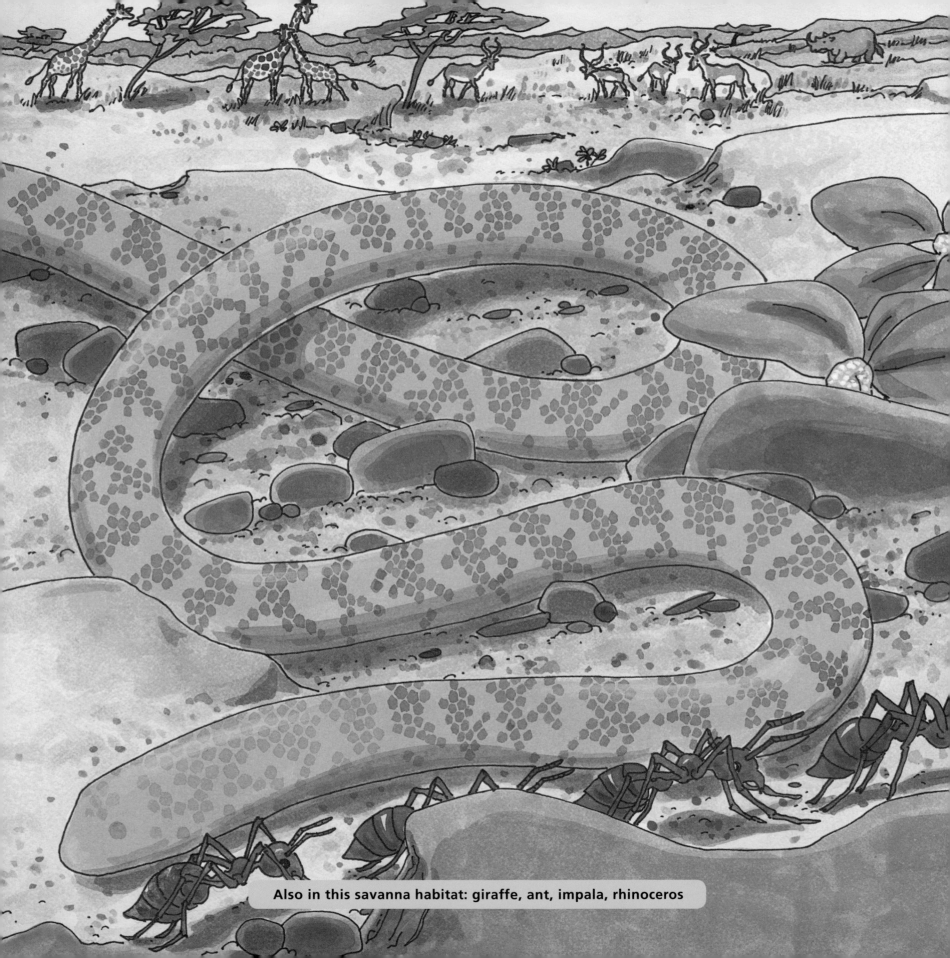

Also in this savanna habitat: giraffe, ant, impala, rhinoceros

Can you guess what kind of snake this is?

Its common name comes from its skin pattern (like a precious stone) and its unique tail (which sounds like a child's toy). It appeared on the first flag of the United States of America during the American Revolution.

The **EASTERN DIAMONDBACK RATTLER** *(Crotalus adamanteus)*
lives in the southeastern United States. It can reach 8 feet
(2.5 m) in length and has the longest fangs of any rattlesnake.
Its fangs normally lie flat against the roof of its mouth
and swing forward to inject deadly venom into its prey.
At the end of its tail is a rattle: a series of horny
segments made of keratin (like our fingernails). Every
time the snake sheds its skin, a new rattle is formed.
These snakes usually have 5 to 10 rattles, but the record
for a snake in captivity is more than two dozen. When
threatened, the snake raises its tail and shakes it. If you
hear a rattle, look out!

Also in this woodland habitat: fox, red-headed woodpecker, deer, raccoon

Can you guess what kind of snake this is?

Its common name comes from the Portuguese word for "snake with hood." It lives in eastern Africa and lays 5 to 15 eggs. Dinner is usually other snakes, small mammals, and birds.

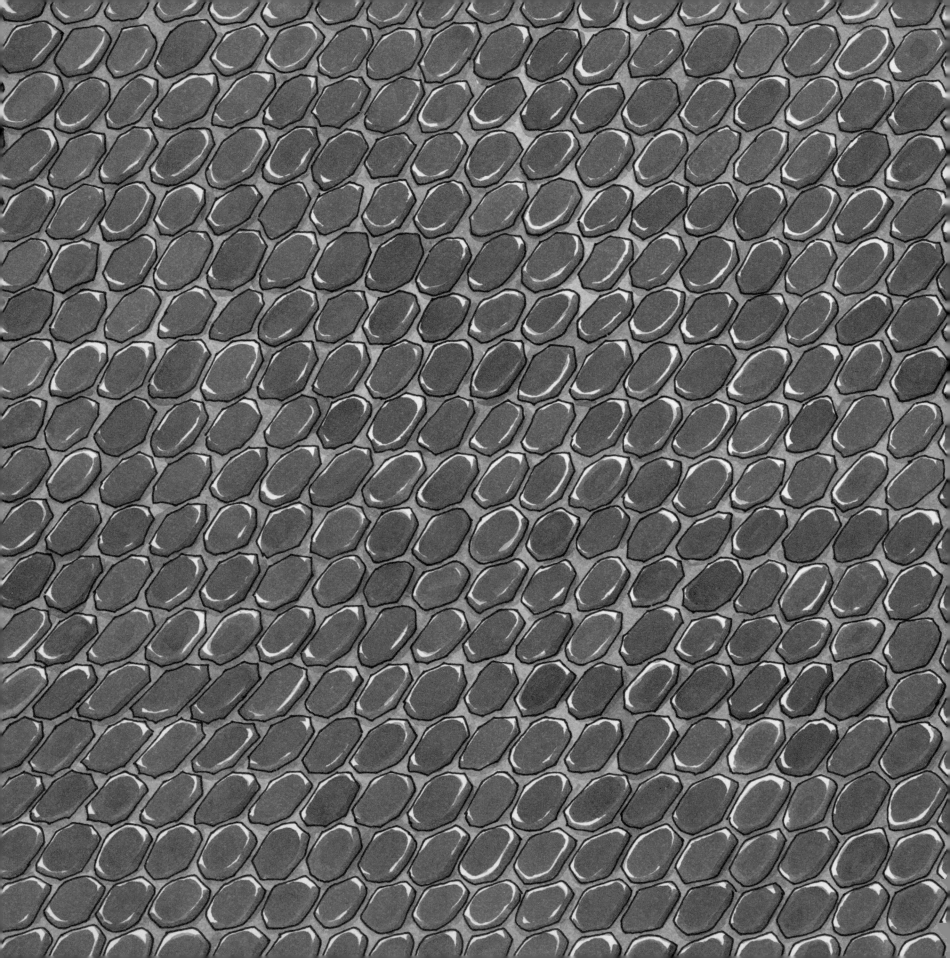

The **RED SPITTING COBRA** *(Naja pallida)* is the most colorful of all cobras, but not the biggest. It can grow to 5 feet (1.5 m) long; and the older it gets, the deeper the red color becomes. If this cobra is alarmed, it will rear up, hiss, and spread its "hood" (flatten its neck) to make itself look bigger. It doesn't actually spit— it sprays venom on enemies from as far away as 6 feet (2 m). If venom gets into your eyes, it can cause severe pain and blindness. This cobra moves pretty fast, even with its head raised. There are 270 kinds of cobras, including some sea snakes, and they are all poisonous.

Also in this grassland habitat: jackel, lion, mouse, hippopotamus

Can you guess what kind of snake this is?

There might be more of this species of snake than any other in the world. The top of its back is black to absorb heat from the sun. Sometimes hundreds, even thousands, of these snakes amass together.

The **YELLOW-BELLIED SEA SNAKE** *(Pelamis platurus)* is found throughout
the world in tropical waters. Often seen in huge groups floating close to the surface,
these snakes will drift along with the current for miles. There are more than 60 species of
sea snakes, but the yellow-bellied sea snake, also called the flat-tail wanderer, is the most
widespread snake on Earth. It can spend up to 3 hours underwater and bears live young
without ever leaving the sea. It has 2 venomous fangs on its top jaw and eats small fish
and eels. The yellow-bellied sea snake's flattened tail acts like a paddle to help it swim
and dive. It can swim backward but can't really move if it is washed up on shore.

Also in this ocean habitat: queen angelfish, sea horse, butterfly fish, sea star

Can you guess what kind of snake this is?

It is one of the world's longest snakes. Its complex, patterned skin, good for camouflage, is famous—in *Shrek*, the ogre used its hanging skins as a room divider, and Crocodile Dundee had a vest made from it.

The **RETICULATED PYTHON** *(Python reticulatus)* lives in the rainforests and woodlands of Southeast Asia. It can grow to more than 28 feet (8.5 m) and weigh more than 300 pounds (136 kg). It is an excellent swimmer but often waits in trees for prey to wander by. A constrictor, it wraps around a pig or deer and squeezes it to death. A large animal may take months to digest. Females can lay 100 eggs at a time, and the mom broods the eggs (coils around the eggs to keep the temperature even)—an unusual behavior for snakes. Hatchlings are 2 to 3 feet (almost a meter) long at birth and immediately become predators, eating small mice, lizards, and frogs. Pythons are often killed by humans, who make vests, pants, and boots from their beautiful skin.

Also in this rainforest habitat: tiger, turtle, water buffalo, tiger swallowtail butterfly

Fun Snake Words

Arboreal: Lives in a tree.

Brumate: Resting in an insulated crevice or burrow during cold weather. Similar to hiberation (but not as long or deep a sleep).

Camouflage: When an animal uses patterns or colors to conceal itself or blend into the background.

Carnivore: A meat eater.

Cold-blooded: An animal whose temperature changes with its surroundings (it can get warmed by the sun or chilled during the winter; it may hibernate until the weather warms up).

Constrictor: A snake that coils or wraps itself around its prey and squeezes it to death by suffocation.

Diurnal: Active during the day.

Habitat: Where the animal lives.

Hibernate: When an animal remains inactive during cold months, often "sleeping" in a burrow or cave.

Keratin: A tough material made of protein found in fingernails, hair, horns, hoofs, and claws.

Live-bearing: Giving birth to fully formed young, not eggs that hatch later.

Migrate: To move from one region to another, usually because of the weather or to forage for food.

Nocturnal: Active at night.

Predator: An animal that hunts and eats other animals.

Reptile: Cold-blooded animals, including snakes, turtles, lizards, and crocodiles.

Scales: Thickened parts of a reptile's skin, usually forming a pattern.

Serpent: An ancient name for a snake or reptile.

Sidewinding: To move sideways in a series of S-shaped curves.

Venomous: Animals that sting or bite and deliver chemicals that can kill or paralyze prey.

Viper: A venomous snake with large, hinged fangs.

Find Out More about Snakes

Books

Mattison, Chris. *The New Encyclopedia of Snakes*. Princeton, NJ: Princeton University Press, 2007.

Mattison, Chris. Rattler!: *A Natural History of Rattlesnakes*. London, UK: Blandford, 1996.

O'Shea, Mark. *Boas and Pythons of the World*. Princeton, NJ: Princeton University Press, 2011.

O'Shea, Mark. *Venomous Snakes of the World*. Princeton, NJ: Princeton University Press, 2005.

Whittley, Sarah. *Snakes*. New York, NY: St. Martin's Press, 2002.

Websites

California Academy of Sciences
www.calacademy.org/academy/exhibits/snakes/

Enchanted Learning—Snakes
www.enchantedlearning.com/subjects/reptiles/snakes/printouts.shtml

Kids' Planet: Defenders of Wildlife
www.kidsplanet.org/factsheets/snakes.html

PBS/Nature
www.pbs.org/wnet/nature/episodes/the-reptiles-snakes/introduction/2908/